LARRY BURKETT

INSURANCE PLANS

MOODY PRESS

CHICAGO

About the Author

Larry Burkett is committed to teaching God's people His principles for managing money. Unfortunately, money management is one area often neglected by Christians, and it is a major cause of conflict and disruption in both business and family life.

For more than two decades Larry has counseled and taught God's principles for finance across the country. As director of Christian Financial Concepts, Larry has counseled, conducted seminars, and written numerous books on the subject of maintaining control of the budget. In additon he is heard on more than 1000 radio outlets worldwide.

Insurance Plans

Christians often ask two questions about insurance: "Is insurance scriptural?" and, "Does owning insurance reflect a lack of faith?" The answers to both are yes and no. Insurance is not specifically defined in Scripture; however, the principle of future provision is. Owning insurance does not necessarily reflect a lack of faith in God, but it is increasingly being used for that reason. Just as damaging are the secondary effects that insurance has on our society: greed, slothfulness, waste, and fear.

Biblical Perspective

A Christian must believe that *all* resources belong to God. Therefore an insurance company's resources are God's. As such, we will be held accountable for how those resources are spent on us just as certainly as if the funds came out of our savings account. "The righteousness of the upright will deliver them, but the treacherous will be caught by their own greed" (Proverbs 11:6).

If members of the Body of Christ understood and accepted their various responsibilities, insurance would be largely unnecessary. As any family had a need, the others would respond accordingly (2 Corinthians 8:14-15). Unfortunately most Christians are not at that point yet and most likely won't be for a while.

With few exceptions, not having insurance reflects not greater faith but rather slothfulness and a lack of planning. It is the same attitude that causes families to live "by faith" and develop no savings while they continue to accumulate debt. (*Financial Freedom* also discusses what the Bible says about debt.) Obviously God may convict an individual to have no insurance on the "assurance" that He will provide. However, the truth of this must be evidenced by his total trust. Remember, God never fails.

God's Word teaches provision, not protection. Insurance can be used to provide where a potential loss would be excessive. This is especially true when another's loss must be considered, as in automobile liability coverage. "A prudent man sees evil and hides himself, the naive proceed and pay the penalty" (Proverbs 27:12).

That point was brought home to me clearly as I sought to insure our ministry buildings. A group of Christians had purchased our property and had given it to us to develop a counseling center. Even minimal insurance coverage turned out to be several thousand dollars a year. After seeking God's will, the answer became clear. Certainly if God was able to provide the buildings initially, He could also replace them if necessary. So the erstwhile insurance money went to buy teaching materials.

"And call upon Me in the day of trouble; I shall rescue you, and you will honor Me" (Psalm 50:15). God does not want us to be foolish; He wants us to be responsible. Too often insurance is used to shift our responsibilities to someone else. Between the government welfare programs and the growth of insurance plans for virtually everything, the Christian community has been duped into believing that we don't need each other. That is a lie from the deceiver to suit his purpose. But when God decides enough is enough, we will again discover the reality of Psalm 73:25. "Whom have I in heaven but Thee? And besides Thee, I desire nothing on earth." Prior to Christ's return, we will again be molded into a working body, and no amount of insurance will be able to buffer us from needing each other. The community plan described in Acts 4:34 will be our insurance plan. That doesn't mean that the use of insurance is unscriptural but that the misuse of it is.

CURRENT ATTITUDES

Why are even Christians tempted to cheat and rationalize their dealings with insurance companies? Several factors are involved. One is that insurance companies seem wealthy and impersonal. Many people believe that the wealthy acquired their wealth dishonestly and therefore are "fair game." Also, since they don't actually know anyone at the insurance company, it's not like cheating an individual.

Another reason is that most Christians expect too much from insurance. They literally expect the insurance company to protect them from every loss. Whenever a Christian gets out of balance with God's

Word, Satan can use fear to direct his actions. God's balance is that we "provide" for our families (1 Timothy 5:8). Satan tells us that we must "protect" them.

Many committed Christians are willing to use insurance funds to do things they would never consider doing with their own money. Recently a Christian physician and I were discussing this issue, and he related an all too common event. He had a Christian patient who was in need of some diagnostic tests. The doctor suggested that she receive the tests as a hospital outpatient because the costs would be substantially less. "Oh, no," she said, "my insurance only pays if I'm admitted to a hospital for at least two days, and I want the best." Certainly that Christian lady would never consider willfully cheating somebody— but didn't she do just that? "And if you have not been faithful in the use of that which is another's, who will give you that which is your own?" (Luke 16:12).

A counselee some time ago told me one of what he called God's "answers" to prayer. His car had been severely damaged in an airport parking lot while he was away on a trip, and unfortunately the "banger" didn't leave a note for the "bangee." Because of the cost, he didn't carry collision insurance to cover the damage, so he drove the car as it was for several weeks. Then one day he was hit from the rear in a multiple-car collision. Although the actual damage from that collision was slight, in getting an estimate for damages, he "neglected" to mention the previous damage done at the airport. Consequently, his car was entirely repaired by the liability insurance of the car that struck him from the rear. "What an answer from the Lord!" he exclaimed.

Unfortunately, that "answer" conflicted with God's Word. "The perverse in heart are an abomination to the Lord, but the blameless in their walk are His delight" (Proverbs 11:20). I simply asked that man to review a few passages of Scripture that dealt with this area, pray about it, ask God's direction, and then do what he thought God wanted him to do. He ended up repaying the insurance company for the original damage.

NET EFFECT OF AN INSURANCE ETHIC

Unfortunately one of the negative side effects of relying so heavily upon insurance as a buffer against every little problem is that we also buffer God's guidance. There is no evidence in Scripture that God promises or desires to buffer His people from every difficulty or inconvenience. In fact, evidence exists that problems are specifically allowed to redirect us or "test" our faith (Romans 5:3; 2 Corinthians 8:2; Philippians 3:7; James 1:3). Thus, when insurance is used in excess, we transfer trust in God to trust in insurance.

The apparently easy access to insurance company funds promotes an attitude of slothfulness both financially and spiritually: financially, there is less incentive to save and anticipate problems; spiritually, there is less need to pray about future needs —of others as well as our own. Those who have access to employer-paid, low deductible insurance plans have a tendency to forget that not everyone in their community has the same opportunity. Legitimate needs within Christian families go unmet because others aren't aware that not everyone can afford the high cost of insurance.

Another net effect of the misuse of insurance is to raise both the cost of insurance and the services that feed off of it. Much of the increased cost of credit is passed on to consumers (including those who pay cash); similarly, the increased cost of insurance abusers is passed on to the diligent. Obviously that discourages conservatism and encourages even more abuses. The tendency is to say, "I want to get my fair share too."

WHAT IS INSURANCE?

Insurance in its simplest form is a plan for surrendering a portion of current resources to offset a future potential loss. This may be related to death, health, accident, theft, and so forth.

In principle, insurance is similar to a farmer's storing grain during the harvest for the winter months. In practice, however, insurance has become a means to protect against every imaginable contingency—and a few that aren't even possible. Used excessively, an unhealthy attitude of dependence on insurance can develop.

Insurance is neither good nor bad, moral nor immoral, but it can be used unwisely and can consume needed funds, rob God, and represent a lack of trust in God. Christians commonly take two extreme views—either you should have no insurance, because it reflects a lack of faith, or you should have so much insurance that your family will never have a financial need.

INDIVIDUAL RESPONSIBILITY

An overwhelmingly simple principle stands out in God's Word: individual responsibility. It really doesn't matter what others are doing. God holds each of us individually responsible for our actions. "But let each one examine his own work, and then he will have reason for boasting in regard to himself alone, and not in regard to another" (Galatians 6:4).

Each Christian must examine every area of his or her daily life frequently to determine if it is up to God's standards. The best quick test is whether or not he or she has peace about his actions.

HEALTH

Health insurance provides a good benefit by making good health care available to most families. Unfortunately, adequate health care is now dependent upon insurance coverage. It costs more to stay one day in a hospital in Idaho than at a fancy hotel in New York City. Christians must use health insurance as we would our own money. Never sign a hospital bill without thoroughly reviewing it. Require documentation for every expenditure. Ask for a reasonable estimate before committing to any health care plan or hospital stay. If you are an employer, check into higher deductible plans that may cost less but provide better catastrophe care. Give incentives to employees who do not abuse the insurance plan.

LIFE

The purpose of any life insurance plan is to provide for those who cannot provide for themselves. Many Christians have too little, but others have too much. It always baffles me to counsel a Christian who has purchased an enormous amount of life insurance to protect a huge estate. "When there is a man who has labored with wisdom, knowledge and skill, then he gives his legacy to one who has not labored with them. This too is vanity and a great evil" (Ecclesiastes 2:21).

On the other end of the spectrum are those who have the ability to provide for their families in case they died unexpectedly but apparently don't think they need to. Both examples reflect disobedience to God's principles. "If a man fathers a hundred children and lives many years, however many they be, but his soul is not satisfied with good things, and he does not even have a proper burial, then I say, 'Better the miscarriage than he'" (Ecclesiastes 6:3).

OTHER INSURANCE

To decide what is the correct balance, a simple test can be used. Can you provide for an unexpected loss yourself? If so, then to pay out money for insurance is a waste of God's resources. Great emotional appeals can be made for protecting everything from the dishwasher to possible termites. At what point should we say enough? That point has been reached when a Christian looks around and finds that trusting God no longer seems necessary for future material needs (Philippians 4:19).

CHOOSING AN AGENT

Much care is needed in the selection of an insurance agent. Before choosing your agent, review the types of insurance available, what is covered, and what you can afford. Then select your agent based on the following conditions:

ASK FOR REFERENCES

Don't deal with a nonprofessional or one who sells insurance part-time. Some of the professional designations that agents may earn to verify their experience and knowledge are Chartered Life Underwriter (CLU), Chartered Financial Consultant (ChFC), and Certified Financial Planner (CFP). Experience counts.

EXPECT COOPERATION

Make sure your agent thoroughly analyzes your insurance needs. Don't tolerate an agent who tries to pressure you into buying more insurance than you can afford or need.

TRY TO FIND A CHRISTIAN

Psalm 1:2 encourages us to walk in the counsel of the godly. If at all possible, use the services of a Christian agent.

The average novice in the area of insurance will need the very best counsel possible. Although there are many good insurance companies that are not listed in the top twenty companies, dealing with a company in the top twenty is usually best for the inexperienced person.

Remember, thoroughly read everything that the company asks you to sign. If you don't understand it, require that the agent or company write it out in language that you can understand. Be sure you understand the policy, its exclusions, and its coverage when you purchase it. Don't wait until you file a claim to find out what it covers.

Life Insurance

The purpose of any life insurance plan is ongoing provision for those under our care after our death. The fact that we don't know exactly when we are going to die and may not have the economic resources saved to provide for our families is justification for insurance.

There are benefits and liabilities associated with any kind of insurance. To make good decisions, you must be able to evaluate your needs versus the costs.

THE BENEFITS OF OWNING INSURANCE

First, you can use insurance to provide for contingent liabilities that otherwise could not be met. For instance, most men need the greatest amount of life insurance when they're young because they have a wife and children at home who probably would not be able to support themselves without a husband and father. So insurance is used to produce the needed income. It is substitute collateral for the wage earner. To repeat Proverbs 27:12, "A prudent man sees evil and hides himself, the naive proceed and pay the penalty." The insured is looking ahead, seeing a potential problem, and providing before it occurs.

Second, insurance frees up surplus funds. Let's assume that a husband makes $25,000 a year. If he dies, the family will need a $25,000 income. If Social Security provides $10,000 a year for dependent care, the family is still $15,000 a year short. Where will the funds come from? It would take approximately $150,000 in assets, invested at 10 percent, to provide the $15,000 needed.

These funds can be provided in one of two ways. One is by saving $150,000, in which case insurance is not necessary. The other is with life insurance. If a family has $150,000 but wants to use it to buy a home, the insurance provides substitute collateral. In other words, it frees $150,000 to be used now or given away if desired.

THE LIABILITIES OF OWNING INSURANCE

One liability of insurance is that it costs money, so you must give up current spending in order to provide for the future. If you need $150,000 of insurance, it will cost money from your current budget.

Another liability of insurance, as previously mentioned, is that it can divert your dependency from God. Solomon wrote, "Trust in the Lord with all your heart, and do not lean on your own understanding. In all your ways acknowledge Him, and He will make your paths straight" (Proverbs 3:5-6). That doesn't mean to forgo all insurance, but it does mean that we are to trust in the Lord, not insurance.

TERM LIFE INSURANCE

Term insurance is insurance that is sold for a determinable number of years. Most term policies do not accumulate any cash reserves, but they provide the largest immediate death protection for your premium dollar. Term insurance is strictly for protection. The death benefits will be paid only if you die while the policy is in effect.

Calculations for term life premiums are based on your actual age. The cost goes up as your age goes up. At a later age, such as fifty or sixty years, term insurance will be significantly more expensive.

A term policy can be "guaranteed renewable" and "convertible." That means that you can continue your insurance at the end of each term without a medical examination simply by paying the increased premium. Renewable term policies commonly can be continued until a certain age, such as seventy, eighty, or even one hundred, when all coverage stops. Convertible term insurance allows you to change to a whole life policy to continue your coverage.

There are two basic types of term insurance—decreasing term and level term. Decreasing term premiums remain the same, but the face value, or face benefit, decreases as prescribed (i.e., annually, every five years, ten years, and so on). The premiums of level term insurance increase while the face value stays the same. Level or decreasing term can be selected for periods ranging from one to thirty years or until age sixty-five.

Which type of term insurance is better for the average family? Level term is better for some families because the need for insurance does not decrease at a predictable rate as the decreasing term policy does. However, the determining factors are need and the amount of money budgeted for insurance.

Term contracts are sold in two basic forms: current assumption and guaranteed premiums. Guaranteed premiums will not increase for the term of the policy, but they may be decreased by the insurance company. Current assumption contracts usually guarantee premiums for a certain number of years, after which they may be increased or decreased as the insurance company deems necessary.

If you are going to buy term insurance, remember these four factors: (1) buy only what you need; (2) be sure it is a renewable policy and will not be canceled because of bad health; (3) make sure it is renewable to at least age one hundred; and (4) compare its cost for a twenty-year period to other kinds of insurance, such as a whole life.

If you determine that term insurance will best fit your needs, seek counsel about the various policies before purchasing one from a professional Christian insurance agent.

You may also find a yearly comparison on insurance companies in *Consumer Reports* and a rating of insurance companies in A. M. Best's books of ratings. You may find both of these publications at your local library, or you can contact A. M. Best at (201) 439-2200 for a catalog of publications.

U.S. News and World Report and *Wall Street Journal* listed the names and phone numbers of some companies that will send you a printout of some competitive term insurance policies at some of the cheapest premiums in the United States. The companies are:

Select Quote, 1-800-343-1985
Term Quote, 1-800-444-8376
Financial Independence Group,
1-800-527-1155

Your local insurance agent may be able to provide competitive term policies. Compare policies and companies, and obtain at least three estimates before buying.

CASH VALUE INSURANCE

Cash value insurance is known as whole life, universal life, variable life, ordinary life, permanent insurance, or any number of other trade names. Its basic feature is that it is usually purchased for an individual's lifetime at a flat rate for the life of the policy and accumulates some cash reserves from the paid-in premiums. As it begins to accumulate a cash value, it will pay interest on the accumulated cash value, and many times the policy will pay dividends (cash returns), which can be used to offset the cost of insurance. The annual cost of whole life insurance starts at a higher rate than for term insurance, but the premiums never increase. The added amount you pay for whole life above the cost of term insurance is a form of savings.

At a younger age, cash value insurance is normally more costly than term. For a young family with limited funds available it represents at best a questionable purchase. At worst cash value insurance can be so costly that many families are forced to buy inadequate amounts of insurance at a time when their need is the greatest.

A whole life policy, like a term policy, may include a waiver of premium disability benefit, accidental death benefit, or both. The premium rate will be higher if these benefits are included.

Under the waiver of premiums benefit, if you become permanently disabled and are unable to pay, the company will pay the premiums. The disability usually must last for at least six months before it will be considered permanent.

The accidental death benefit provision promises to pay an additional sum equal to the face value of the policy if the death occurs by accidental means. The accidental death benefit is often called "double indemnity" because you receive double the face value.

Premiums for cash value policies are classified as either "participating" (par) or "nonparticipating" (nonpar). Policies with participating premiums are marketed by stock insurance and mutual insurance companies that may offer dividends to policyholders. Dividends payable on participating policies represent a rebate on the premium you pay for your policy and may vary from year to year depending upon the company's costs.

UNIVERSAL LIFE INSURANCE

Universal life, sometimes called "complete" or "total" life insurance, is a combination of term insurance and a tax-deferred savings account that pays a flexible interest rate. The interest rate usually reflects current market rates and is much higher than that guaranteed on savings from traditional policies. It is a policy that is broken down into three parts—death benefit, administrative costs, and savings. Premiums may be paid at any time and for any amount above a minimum and can be flexible or level, but eventually they may not be required if enough money is accumulated in the savings portion to pay the mortality and administrative costs for the life expectancy of the insured.

A universal life insurance policy is normally sold by agents on the basis of how much you will accumulate by age sixty-five in the savings portion. This tactic sells life insurance as an investment, not as insurance to provide for dependents at your death. (*Sound Investments* discusses wise ways to invest your money.)

If you know you will need life insurance in your seventies and eighties, a universal life policy may be preferable to term insurance. The need for insurance at ages seventy and eighty is normally due to poor planning and a lack of discipline while one is young or possibly due to some unique estate planning requirements. You will not realize the stated return on the universal life policy printout until you have been paying on it for approximately fifteen to twenty years. Any cancellation prior to this time will cost you dearly compared to purchasing term insurance and investing the difference in a tax deferred vehicle.

VARIABLE LIFE INSURANCE

A variable life policy is considered a security and is sold by prospectus. The death benefit and cash value go up or down depending on the yield or security funds you select from the company's investment plans. A variable policy offers loan privileges, optional rides, and surrender and exchange rights just as whole life policies do.

These new policies offer higher returns, but they also mean greater risk for policyholders. Returns can change drastically from year to year.

SINGLE PREMIUM LIFE INSURANCE

Single premium life insurance in the past was a popular tax-deferred accumulation plan or vehicle to gain tax-free income. Although tax law changes have drastically curtailed its attractiveness as a tax-free income vehicle, it may still be an alternative as a tax-deferred accumulation plan with some death benefits. Contact your insurance agent for the accurate tax law consequences surrounding this policy and to find out whether it meets your insurance needs.

The insurance industry is constantly changing in response to tax law revisions. New products will be created to reflect these new tax laws. If you want to research the various types of policies on the market, contact your insurance agent. This booklet only provides a brief summary of the most popular types of insurance policies available.

CREDIT OR MORTGAGE LIFE INSURANCE

A credit or mortgage life insurance policy is decreasing term life insurance sold in connection with home, auto, or other credit extensions. This type of policy is designed to relieve survivors of economic strain by paying off the deceased's outstanding loan balance. (Credit disability insurance covers monthly payments if you are disabled.)

Rather than buying several of these small, relatively expensive policies, it would be wiser to incorporate these needs into your overall life and disability insurance planning and purchase a single policy.

POLICY PROVISIONS

When you buy a life insurance policy, the company agrees to pay a sum of money upon your death or retirement. You agree to pay a specified premium regularly. The grace period allows thirty days to elapse during which time the premium may be paid without penalty. A lapsed policy may be put back in force (reinstated) if it has not been turned in for cash. To reinstate a policy, the policyholder must again qualify as an acceptable risk and pay overdue premiums with interest.

An important provision in every policy is the naming of the beneficiary. You can name one or more persons as contingent beneficiaries who will receive your policy proceeds if the primary beneficiary dies before you do. Your right to make changes in the beneficiary arrangement should be included in your application for the policy.

Is Insurance a Good Way to Save?

An argument for cash value policies is that they are a means of forced savings. This is true to some extent, but the difficulty with using insurance as a savings plan is that when the cash value is borrowed, the death benefits are reduced. Hence the family may be left without enough provision.

When evaluating insurance as a way to save money, you need to understand several facts. First, there are two components to a cash value policy's interest rate or earnings: the actual guaranteed rate and the projected rate, or dividend. The guaranteed earnings are typically between 3 and 5 percent.

Second, the quoted interest is probably before administrative fees and commissions are subtracted. Therefore, your net earnings will not be as much.

Third, keep in mind that the interest rates are adjusted annually, if not more frequently.

Most of God's people have little reason not to be disciplined enough to save the reserves they need for emergencies or future needs. As a short-term investment, the savings in most insurance policies draw less than half the interest that could be earned elsewhere. It is a high price to pay for a lack of discipline.

Proverbs 19:20-21 tells us, "Listen to counsel and accept discipline, that you may be wise the rest of your days. Many are the plans in a man's heart, but the counsel of the Lord, it will stand."

How Much Insurance Is Enough?

"There is a grievous evil which I have seen under the sun: riches being hoarded by their owner to his hurt" (Ecclesiastes 5:13). "How much is enough?" is a difficult question to answer precisely. There are many variables within each family that must be considered, such as the age of the children, the wife's income capability, existing debts, current lifestyle and income, and any other sources of after-death income besides life insurance. One person may wish to supply enough insurance proceeds for his family to live off interest income alone, whereas another may wish to provide enough for a specific number of years.

These decisions are important and should be made mutually by husband and wife.

A typical family's insurance needs begin when the first child is conceived and reach a maximum when the last child is conceived. The need for insurance increases again when the children are grown and out of the home before the wife has reached sixty-two years of age. Social Security will not provide death benefits for the wife until age sixty-two.

Insurance needs drop to zero at retirement age when the couple has accumulated debt-free assets, investments, and adequate retirement savings. Therefore, an insurance policy should provide a maximum amount of protection while the family is growing and taper off as the family gets older and smaller.

LIFE INSURANCE NEEDS WORKSHEET

Present Income Per Year		_____
		Line 1
Payments No Longer Required		
Estimated Living Cost		
(for Husband)	_____	
Life Insurance	_____	
Savings	_____	
Investments	_____	
Taxes	_____	
_____	_____	
_____	_____	
	Total =	_____
		Line 2
INCOME REQUIRED		
TO SUPPORT FAMILY	(Line 1 - Line 2) =	_____
		Line 3
INCOME AVAILABLE		
Social Security	_____	
Wife's Income	_____	
Retirement Plans	_____	
Investments	_____	
_____	_____	
	Total =	_____
		Line 4
ADDITIONAL INCOME REQUIRED		
TO SUPPORT FAMILY	(Line 3 - Line 4) =	_____
		Line 5
INSURANCE REQUIRED TO		
PROVIDE NEEDED INCOME		
(Invested at 10% interest)	(Line 5 x 10) =	_____
		Line 6
LUMP SUM REQUIREMENTS		
Debt Payments	_____	
Funeral Costs	_____	
Estate Tax & Settlement Costs	_____	
Education Costs	_____	
_____		
	Total =	_____
		Line 7

Life Insurance

TOTAL FUNDS REQUIRED   (Line 6 -
Line 7) = _____
Line 8

ASSETS AVAILABLE
Real Estate   _____
Stock and Bonds   _____
Savings   _____

Total = _____
Line 9

TOTAL INSURANCE NEEDED   (Line 8 -
Line 9) = _____

BUDGETING FOR INSURANCE

The next question is, How much can you afford? Insurance costs should constitute approximately 6 percent of your net spendable income. Net spendable income is the balance after you have paid tithes and taxes. This excludes house or automobile insurance and includes life insurance, health insurance, disability, and so on. (The 6 percent figure assumes that those who have health insurance are part of a group plan.)

If you are not part of a group health insurance plan, this percentage of your budget will increase. Therefore, both life insurance and health insurance must be selected and budgeted carefully. If you increase the insurance area of your budget from 6 percent to 10 percent, there is no alternative but to decrease another area of your budget in order to make it balance. (For more tips on setting up a budget, see *Personal Finances* in this series.)

THINGS TO AVOID WHEN BUYING LIFE INSURANCE

Many times we are talked into buying what we do not want instead of what we need. This generally happens because we don't know what to avoid. The following checklist of things to avoid when selecting life insurance may be helpful:

1. Avoid the double indemnity clause. Most people don't die by accident, and you should have the amount of insurance your family needs without depending on your dying in an accident.

2. Forget the premium waiver, under which the insurance company pays your premiums if you become permanently disabled. It is a large expense for a small benefit.

3. Don't be sold insurance; be intelligent. Learn to buy what you need rather than what somebody else wants you to have.

POINTERS FOR POLICYHOLDERS

1. Keep your company informed of your address. Each year a number of policyholders move without notifying their insurance companies, risking accidental lapsing of their policies.

2. Read your life insurance policy. Your agent should be willing to help you. Be sure that you understand the basic provisions and benefits.

3. Keep your policy in a safe place. You can get a duplicate policy if it is lost or destroyed by fire but not without some inconvenience and delay. As an additional safeguard, keep a separate record of your policies. Be sure that your beneficiary knows where a copy of your policy is kept. Generally policies must be sent to the company when you file for benefits. If you keep your policies in a safe deposit box, your beneficiary may have to obtain permission to open the box after your death.

4. Discuss your insurance program with your family or other beneficiaries.

5. Review your life insurance program with your agent once a year or when a major event occurs (birth, death, marriage, divorce).

NO INSURANCE

God may direct some people not to have life insurance or any other after-death provision, but any decision to be without insurance should not be made unilaterally. Both husband and wife should be in total accord, praying about it, and seeking God's peace first. If you have any doubts, go ahead and buy the insurance. You can always cancel it later if necessary.

MORE QUESTIONS ABOUT LIFE INSURANCE

HOW SHOULD ONE HANDLE LIFE INSURANCE BENEFITS?

After you buy the life insurance, you must decide how the funds will be handled when paid to the beneficiary. The proceeds from life insurance are not usually subject to federal or state income taxes. In other words, you don't have to pay income taxes on the money received from life insurance. If it is put into an estate, it may be subject to probate costs, and estate taxes may be required, depending on the total value of the deceased's estate and the ownership of the life insurance policy. If life insurance proceeds are taken as income rather than a lump sum, interest is included in each payment. The interest portion is taxable.

If the proceeds are invested, the income can be subject to federal and state income tax, just as any other generated income, but it depends on your total taxable income and where the funds are invested.

Families with large estates need to seek estate planning help from a good estate planning attorney to ensure that the estate taxes and probate costs are minimized. This would be particularly valuable should the husband and wife die in an accident, causing the probate costs and the inheritance taxes to be maximized.

Use a simple testamentary trust to handle the funds in the event of a common death. A testamentary trust is set up in your will to direct how the insurance proceeds will be invested upon the death of the insured.

SHOULD A HUSBAND LEAVE HIS LIFE INSURANCE IN TRUST FOR HIS WIFE?

A husband and wife should talk about after-death preparation. Some of that discussion will include what the wife will do with the insurance money that the husband will leave at his death. Most husbands are concerned that someone will come along and trick their wives out of their money because they basically understand nothing about money. Therefore, they plan to leave it in trust for their wives where only the income can be spent and used only for the wife's personal benefit.

However, two things are wrong with that reasoning. First, if a wife doesn't understand anything about money, she should learn. It doesn't matter that she doesn't want to learn or that her husband doesn't want her to. God says she should. Husbands and wives are to be one in the Lord. In order to give good counsel to her husband, the wife has to have a knowledge of finances. Statistically, 85 percent of husbands will predecease their wives. For the wife not to be trained in the area of finances is nothing more than both spouses sticking their heads in the sand. A wife must be trained in the area of finances and be fully aware of the couple's financial situation.

Second, if you are committing these assets, including the income, to a trust that can only be used for your widow, it is unscriptural. If your wife remarries, she is bound to her new husband, and they are to be one.

Whatever assets she has should also be available to him. If they are to be one, there can be no barrier between them.

There is basically nothing wrong with leaving assets in trust for a wife if it is a good financial planning tool. For instance, if the husband and wife were killed in a common accident and the funds were left stating that the income should be paid to the wife as long as she is alive and then upon her death pay the income to the children, or give the principal to the Lord's work, you might save some taxes.

SHOULD WIVES HAVE LIFE INSURANCE?

Over the last few years, the wife has become almost an equal wage earner in many families. If your family is dependent on your wife's salary, you probably need to insure her as well because if for some reason she is injured or dies, the family would be in deep financial trouble, possibly losing your home, cars, and virtually everything else you own.

First, determine if you can afford the extra insurance. If funds are limited, you need to insure the primary wage earner, usually the husband. If there is sufficient money, it may be logical to put insurance on the wife. Typically the earnings of a wife will only be critical to the family while small children are at home. Therefore, the older she gets, the less the need for insurance.

SHOULD CHILDREN HAVE LIFE INSURANCE?

There are two logical reasons to have insurance on your children—for burial expenses and to guarantee the insurability of your children in later years. Actually insurance on the children is only necessary if you need it to cover the cost of burial, because only a small fraction of people are uninsurable at the time they marry.

IS LIFE INSURANCE A GOOD WAY TO LEAVE MONEY TO THE CHURCH?

In our generation many Christian insurance agents recommend that Christians purchase an insurance policy and give it to their local church. In other words, rather than giving some money to the church immediately, they suggest that you buy cash value life insurance, donate it to the church, make the payments (which are deductible), and when you die the church inherits the face value of the policy.

Let's examine this policy from two perspectives—assets and liabilities.

One asset is that it forces you to save to leave something to the local church. The second asset is that if you died soon, the church would get the money and you wouldn't have to make many payments.

Now what are the liabilities? First, the insurance company makes a profit off the insurance policy that you buy. Therefore, you're giving part of the money that would go to the church to an insurance company. Second, relatively speaking it's an expensive method of leaving money to the local church, and there is no guarantee that any church will be the same in ten or twenty years, should you live that long. Proverbs 27:1 says, "Do not boast about tomorrow, for you do not know what a day may bring forth." In other words, if you're going to give to God's kingdom, do your giving now. Don't put the money into an insurance policy with your church as the beneficiary. (*Giving and Tithing*, a booklet in this series, explains positive ways to give to the church.)

WHAT ABOUT LIFE INSURANCE FOR SINGLES?

Single people who have no financial dependents probably do not need life insurance. Remember, the purpose of life insurance is to provide for someone after your death for whom you are providing while you are alive.

CONCLUSIONS

Probably the best way to determine the type of life insurance you should buy is to consider two factors: (1) the amount you need, and (2) the amount you can afford. When you talk about selecting the right kind of insurance, you must consider not only the current annual cost but its cost during the next twenty years. Shop for the policy that best fits your individual needs at the lowest cost. You can probably get the best value by purchasing term insurance and saving the difference in a deferred or tax-free investment.

However, the practical truth is that most people don't save the difference; they spend it. When they get to be fifty or older, their term insurance can become prohibitively expensive. Buy term if you can't afford whole life, but if by the age of thirty-five you have not been self-disciplined enough to save the difference that the cash value would have cost, then convert to a whole life plan.

Health Insurance

In our generation health insurance is a basic need. Few families can afford the cost of a single hospital stay. Medical insurance for most of us represents good, logical planning. It provides a valuable benefit by making good health care available to most families.

The matter of health insurance is too complex to do more than touch on it here. By understanding this brief and general information about what coverage is available and what to consider when buying health insurance, you will be able to evaluate what type of coverage fits your need.

TYPES OF HEALTH INSURANCE

Each type of basic insurance covers different health care expenses. There are two basic types of health insurance—basic coverage and major medical. Hospital, surgical, and general medical expenses are basic coverages. The benefits paid are limited to a certain amount. Major medical and comprehensive insurance offer broad coverage and high maximum benefits. There is usually a deductible paid by the insured.

BASIC COVERAGE

Hospitalization covers daily and miscellaneous expenses when a person is in the hospital. Daily expenses include room and board and nursing charges. Miscellaneous expenses cover services such as X rays, drugs, lab examinations, dressings, and physical therapy.

Surgical expense provides coverage for surgery fees for operations performed in or out of the hospital. Some policies pay only a maximum amount as listed on a relative value table, but a preferred policy will pay according to the usual, customary, and reasonable expense. Surgeons charge different rates, and your policy should pay the rates charged in your community.

General medical covers any doctor's visits in or out of the hospital that do not involve surgery. Diagnostic and laboratory tests may also be included. A general medical policy is limited. Find out how much it pays per visit, how many visits it will pay, and whether the policy covers house calls and office visits.

MAJOR MEDICAL

Major medical insurance pays a major share of the cost of treatment and is basically catastrophic coverage. It includes hospital, surgical, and other medical treatment not covered by the basic policies. A major medical policy normally covers a percentage (75 to 80 percent) of all expenses above a deductible. The deductible is the amount of medical expenses you must pay before your insurance company starts paying. You also pay the remaining 20 to 25 percent of the expenses. This is commonly called "coinsurance" because you share the burden of the medical bill with your insurance company. Coinsurance may encourage the insured to keep costs at a minimum.

A policy may feature a "stop-loss" provision that limits the amount that you have to pay. For example, your policy may state that after you have paid $1,500 of your own (out-of-pocket) money, the insurer will pay the rest of your medical expenses.

A policy may pay you only a limited amount of total expenses each year. In some policies a part of the benefits is reinstated when the patient has gone six to twelve months without a recurrence of the particular illness. In other words, it is reinstated every calendar year.

Most health insurance policies expect you to pay a portion of your expenses—the deductible. The deductible paid by the insured may be any amount—from $1 to $1,000. The higher the deductible, the less you pay in premiums. If you can't afford the health insurance you'd like, it would be wise to purchase a major medical policy with a high deductible. This would cover you for a serious illness or accident. The money you save in premiums could be used for minor health care.

DISABILITY INSURANCE

Psalm 37:25 says, "I have been young, and now I am old; yet I have not seen the righteous forsaken, or his descendants begging bread." As we have learned, there is nothing wrong with insurance when it is used to provide out of our own resources. Disability insurance provides you with an income in the event you are disabled and unable to work. Although a temporary transition fund may well be necessary, covering yourself against the contingency can easily get out of balance.

If you are subject to Social Security taxes, then you already have some disability provision. Disability benefit payments are paid on employees that pay Social Security taxes and are based on the employee's level of earnings over a period of years. Benefits pay only if your disability is expected to last for more than twelve months. Check this out to see if it's sufficient.

Keep in mind that Social Security has been determined by the Supreme Court of the United States not to be an insurance plan but social welfare provided by the government. Whether you accept Social Security disability will depend upon your convictions on government-provided welfare.

Many employers provide a form of disability protection through a group plan. Find out if your employer offers this coverage. Normally, disability benefits are paid on a percentage of the insured's regular gross income. Most policies require total disability before benefits are paid, but sometimes you can collect on partial disability if a period of total disability follows for the same cause. When reviewing a policy, determine its definition of disability since each policy contains its own definition. The best definition would be one stating that you are unable to perform the main duties of "your occupation." The worst definition would state "any occupation."

Other options provide for payments to begin after a set waiting period (thirty days, sixty days, and so on) after the beginning of disability. The longer you wait, the lower your premiums. You must also choose whether benefits will be paid for one year, two years, five years or until age sixty-five. Again, the shorter the time of disability coverage, the lower your premiums.

GROUP OR INDIVIDUAL POLICY?

Health insurance policies may be purchased through a group plan or on an individual basis from an insurance company. Employers offer group health insurance coverage to their employees as a "fringe benefit." Premiums under a group plan are usually lower than those for individual coverage. The employer may pay all or part of the premium.

Individual health insurance policies are those you buy yourself through an agent. You choose the benefits you want. The premiums will be based on your age, sex, and physical condition, as well as the amount of coverage you choose. The premiums are higher than for similar group coverage. Shopping around for cost and value is important with health insurance. You will find that costs for virtually identical polices may vary as much as 50 percent from one major insurance company to another.

HEALTH MAINTENANCE ORGANIZATIONS (HMOs)

In America we use doctors and hospitals primarily as firemen. We wait until we have a fire and then call someone to put it out. We don't take good care of ourselves, many of us don't eat right, certainly we aren't getting enough exercise, and we're under so much stress that our bodies are breaking down. So we go to the doctor and want him to give us a pill to get over it. Health Maintenance Organizations have developed as a result of this fix-me-up mentality.

HMOs negotiate with major employers to take care of all their health care needs from obstetrics to surgery to minor care, but the employers have to use the HMO's doctors, hospitals, and clinics. The employer or individual enrolls as a member by paying a fee that covers all medical expenses from office visits to long-term hospitalization. The premiums are so low that members will seek out medical care before major treatment is needed. This prepaid health care is based on preventive care.

A NEW FORM OF INSURANCE

A new concept in health care insurance is available only to Christians who attend church regularly and neither smoke nor drink and sign a statement to that effect. This particular plan is based on the principles taught by the apostle Paul in 2 Corinthians 8:14-15: "At this present time your abundance being a supply for their want, that their abundance also may become a supply for your want, that there may be equality; as it is written, 'He who gathered much did not have too much, and he who gathered little had no lack.'" In other words, those with a surplus help those with a lack.

The plan works like this. You join an association of Christians agreeing to care for each other. Those who have a medical expense send the paid receipts to the association. The members of the association are then notified of the cost, and the individual is reimbursed. You basically pay the other members' expenses. Information concerning one such organization may be obtained by writing to: Brotherhood Newsletter, 6680 Taylor Road, Clinton, OH 44216-9033, (216) 825-3656.

The concept offered by this type of association appears to be biblical; however, understand that Christian Financial Concepts is neither associated with nor do we endorse any specific plan. You should evaluate any association's financial management and integrity before joining.

MEDICAID

Medicaid is a government-sponsored program that pays medical bills for low-income people who can't afford the costs of medical care. The strict guidelines for eligibility can be obtained from your local public health or welfare office.

Before looking into this type of health insurance, every Christian needs to address the basic issue of his or her convictions about government welfare. Because of the high cost of medical care, many Medicaid patients are actually forced to leave the hospital before they are well. When their benefits run out, the government puts the doctor under a great deal of pressure to move these patients out of the hospital. This is poor medicine. We are basically getting what we pay for, and when the government pays for health care services, the patient often gets inadequate health care.

Welfare is clearly biblical, but the fact that the government has assumed the function of caring for the poor does not negate our responsibility. With the best of intentions, our welfare system traps people at the lowest economic level by indiscriminate giving. On the other hand, biblical welfare meets needs and always looks toward restoring the individual to a position of productivity. When we allow the needy to become dependent upon the government, they stop looking to God to supply their needs.

MEDICARE

Medicare is the government-sponsored health insurance program for most people sixty-five and older and for some people who are disabled. Medicare is a two-part program.

Part A provides hospital benefits for short-term illness and some benefits for care in a skilled nursing facility or at home. Those who are not automatically eligible pay a monthly premium that is adjusted every year.

Part B is optional medical insurance available for a small fee each month. You may have the premium automatically deducted from your Social Security benefit check if you receive one. This coverage pays most of your medical and surgical fees. Part B is an excellent value because it is inexpensive and gives you at least some help with doctor's fees and other medical costs.

Is Medicare supplemental insurance a good buy? Medicare supplemental insurance is designed to take up where Medicare leaves off. It is a relatively new, often misunderstood, type of health insurance.

The Medicare supplemental insurance right now is relatively inexpensive for the amount of insurance it provides. For instance, heart surgery could cost well above $50,000. The difference between what Medicare pays and the patient's cost could be more than $10,000, which could totally wipe out his savings. Therefore, it may be worth $50 per month/$600 per year to provide for that contingency.

WHAT IF YOU CAN'T AFFORD INSURANCE?

This is a common question about the cost of any kind of insurance but especially the cost of health insurance. If someone is not covered by a group health insurance plan and can't afford an individual health policy or major medical plan, then God's people have to provide for his or her basic needs. That doesn't mean that God can't provide. I've seen God provide for people who didn't have insurance, but when you don't have insurance you take a large risk.

Search for an inexpensive major medical plan with a high deductible that will pay for catastrophic illnesses. You may consider taking this insurance plan to your Christian employer and asking if the company will pick up the cost. If not, go to your church fellowship and present the plan as a legitimate need. If, however, they do not respond by providing the money for the health insurance, you and your spouse should pray about it and decide whether you are where God wants you to be.

If you are willing to try to pay your medical and dental bills, most medical professionals will be happy to try to work something out with you. You may be able to clean their offices or find another way to work off what is owed. Do not avoid or run away from medical bills. God will help you find a way to handle them.

CONCLUSIONS

When planning your health insurance program, be sure the coverage fits your needs and your budget. Examine your policy carefully. Know which expenses are covered by your insurance and which are not. Don't duplicate coverage. Some companies will not pay if another policy is in force for the same coverage. Look over your policy every few years to make sure it fits your family's current needs. Be sure you are covered against major expenses when funds are limited. Compare policies and costs. Remember, they vary greatly from one company to another.

Home Owner's Insurance

A home owner's insurance policy is a comprehensive insurance plan covering everything that could happen to your home, its contents, and liability from almost anything—fire, theft, water, hail, or wind damage. Usually a home owners' policy is the least expensive way to insure a dwelling.

When purchasing home owner's insurance, you need to be aware of the difference between actual cash value insurance versus guaranteed (true) replacement value on your contents or structure. "Actual cash value" refers to the depreciated value of the items, whereas "guaranteed replacement" means your contents and structure will be 100 percent replaced. A guaranteed replacement value insurance policy is worth considering when buying home owner's insurance, even with its increased premiums.

DWELLING INSURANCE

Dwelling insurance is not as comprehensive as a home owner's policy but is often as expensive. It is used to cover those nonowner-occupied dwellings and homes that because of age, condition, or location are not insurable under home owner's policies. There are three basic forms of a dwelling policy—basic, broad, and special.

RENTER'S INSURANCE

The purpose of renter's insurance is threefold. It covers the value of your furniture for replacement and the liability if someone is hurt as a result of your negligence or the negligence of your children. An example is if someone falls over a toy or slips outside of your home. The third purpose is to protect you against a suit from the owner's insurance company for damage to the property. Generally, content coverage and liability insurance are reasonable.

Any insurance needs to be balanced on a need-versus-cost basis. If you can afford to replace all of your household furniture or cover a liability suit resulting from fire or water damage or from negligence, you don't need renter's insurance. But if you cannot, renter's insurance represents good stewardship by spending a small amount to avoid a large contingent liability.

In addition to the types of insurance to cover your home, other options are condo insurance, mobile home insurance, or business owner policies for apartment complexes. See your agent for more details about the type of policy that best fits your needs.

PRIVATE MORTGAGE INSURANCE

Lenders require private mortgage insurance for loans, usually in excess of 80 percent of the purchase price. This insurance can be misleading to the consumer because it is really insurance that protects the lender in case of default by the borrower. However, the borrower pays for it. The premium is usually a percentage of the loan value broken down into monthly increments and is determined by the insurance company's loss experience ratio.

UMBRELLA LIABILITY INSURANCE

An umbrella liability policy provides additional liability coverage over and above the liability limits on your auto or home owner's insurance policies.

The principle here is twofold. One is risk, and the other is balance according to God's Word. In other words, the potential risk of being sued for a million dollars as the result of an automobile accident or as the result of injuries sustained on your property must be balanced against trusting God. Although the probability of getting sued is fairly high in our society, there is no way that we can insure against every contingency. First, it's too costly, and second, it's not trusting God to provide for those needs. So where is the balance?

Statistically, few home owners are going to get sued and lose a suit for a million dollars, but if you have a large net worth and your occupation is one with a lot of public exposure, it can be wise to cover yourself for additional limits in our current "suit happy" society. Automobile drivers run a higher risk of getting sued for a million dollars than most home owners.

You can usually purchase a million-dollar limit policy for less than the annual premium on your home owner's insurance. To qualify, you are normally required to increase your auto and home owner's liability limits first. If you have a lot of assets and don't want to risk them, this premium is not too high a price to pay for a million dollars' worth of coverage.

Automobile Insurance

Clearly the cost of insurance is a major expense and is skyrocketing. Most states require you to carry liability insurance on your car. This type of policy will cover the costs of an accident to other persons and vehicles. Even if your state does not require it, you should at least carry liability insurance because the risk is great and the cost is relatively small. One "at fault" accident can put you into debt for the rest of your life. Remember Proverbs 22:3. Be prudent.

FULL COVERAGE

Full coverage on a vehicle includes all basic coverages—bodily injury, liability, property damage, medical payments, collision, comprehensive, and uninsured motorists. If you have a new car, you should consider carrying full coverage. (For information on buying a car, see *Major Purchases*.)

BODILY INJURY LIABILITY

This type of insurance pays for injuries or deaths to people in other vehicles, in your car, or pedestrians as the result of an accident involving your car for which you are legally liable—whether you are driving or another is driving your vehicle with your permission.

Coverage under this type of policy is referred to in terms of 15/30, with the first number being the amount in thousands that the policy will pay for one person and the second number being the total amount in thousands that it will pay for all persons involved in an accident.

PERSONAL INJURY PROTECTION

This will pay benefits to injured persons for medical expenses, lost wages, substitute services if someone is unable to take care of his or her household, and death, no matter whose fault the accident was. This protection is in effect whether a person is riding in or on your vehicle, getting in or out of it, or is struck as a pedestrian.

Automobile Insurance

PROPERTY DAMAGE LIABILITY

This portion of the insurance policy covers damage to property (houses, buildings, fences, livestock, and any other property belonging to someone else) caused by your car. The terms of coverage are expressed as 15/30/10. The insurance company will pay a maximum of the amount expressed in thousands for (1) each person injured, (2) each accident, and (3) property damage.

MEDICAL PAYMENTS

Medical payments coverage applies to medical expenses resulting from accidental injury to anyone riding in your automobile or struck as a pedestrian.

COLLISION INSURANCE

Collision insurance pays for damages to your vehicle, but not the other person's, when you are involved in a collision. Usually, a deductible is written with this coverage. The company will only pay the market value of your car in case of an accident. For example, your four-year-old compact car might sustain $2,500 in damages in an accident according to an adjuster. However, if the car's market value is only $500, you will receive $500, less your deductible. Therefore, if your vehicle is an older model (more than three years old), you can save money on car insurance by dropping the collision insurance.

If you can afford to pay for repair damages to your vehicle, you can "self-insure" your car. Since collision insurance is relatively expensive, you can put aside the value of the car into an interest-bearing savings account to be used in the event your car is damaged. However, if you cannot afford to save to repair the automobile, you need to obtain collision insurance on your newer vehicle.

COMPREHENSIVE PHYSICAL DAMAGE INSURANCE

This type of coverage provides for the replacement of glass and losses resulting from anything except collision, such as fire, theft, vandalism, and hail. It is relatively inexpensive, and generally the things that are covered are the same regardless of the car's age. Make the decision about this type of insurance according to your budget. If the cost is prohibitively high for your income, you should carry liability only. But before dropping your comprehensive or collision insurance, realize that often the difference can be easily recouped by shopping for the lowest rate of insurance.

UNINSURED MOTORISTS

This type of protection pays for injuries to you and your family caused by a hit-and-run driver or one who doesn't have liability insurance.

OTHER COVERAGES

Also available is death and dismemberment insurance, which provides benefits to you or your family in the event of a death or loss of limb as the result of an automobile accident. Towing insurance pays part or all of the towing charges if your car breaks down. Rental car reimbursement provides you with a car to drive while yours is being repaired.

No Automobile Insurance— Faith or Foolishness?

Proverbs 27:12 has the answer to this question. It says, "A prudent man sees evil and hides himself, the naive proceed and pay the penalty." If you do not look ahead to see the evil and protect yourself, you will end up paying a penalty. In most states in our country to drive without liability insurance on your car is not just bad judgment—it is also illegal. You can go to jail for it, and they can take your house and your car if you hit somebody and can't pay. The choice is to obey or willfully disobey the law.

Liability insurance protects those who might be injured as a result of an accident you caused. In reality, it is the other people who are living by faith, not the person driving without insurance, because they are the ones taking the risk whenever they leave their driveway.

AUTO INSURANCE FOR TEENS

Whether a teenager owns a car or not, the issue of insurance must be addressed. Almost every insurance company will raise the parents' insurance rates as soon as their son or daughter is sixteen because they know the parents are typically going to let their teenager drive a car. This will happen to some extent even if the child is not on their policy.

It is much cheaper for you to add a teenager to your insurance policy than to purchase a separate policy. Limiting teenagers to a small percentage of the total use of the family car can lower your rates.

Remember what Proverbs 29:17 says: "Correct your son, and he will give you comfort; he will also delight your soul." Since most parents use their teenagers to shuttle other children back and forth, you need to set some fundamental rules for the use of the automobile: driving, paying for the car, buying the insurance, and maintenance. Don't wait until your children become teenagers. It's an issue that should be faced while your children are young.

HOW TO SAVE ON AUTOMOBILE INSURANCE COSTS

We've already seen that the age of your car and your ability to "self-insure" can reduce insurance costs, but taking advantage of discounts will also reduce the cost of the insurance. Discounts are offered for:

1. good students with a B average or above

2. drivers who have successfully completed a driver's education course
3. those who take advantage of a carpool
4. multicar families
5. students away at college
6. cars with air bags
7. antitheft devices
8. senior citizens
9. farmers
10. defensive drivers
11. nonsmokers or nondrinkers
12. female, aged thirty to sixty-four as the sole driver in the household

You should check with your insurance agent to see if you qualify for any of these discounts.

A family can save money by avoiding traffic violations. Drunk driving, speeding, or ignoring traffic signs puts points on your driving record and adds dollars to your premiums. The type of automobile has an effect on your premiums. Sporty or fancy cars usually have higher premiums. Be sure to let your agent know immediately when circumstances change within your family. Review your coverage annually.

Other Types of Insurance Coverage

Nursing Home Insurance

The enormous expense of nursing home care is a common problem in today's society. The majority of older people today are in retirement homes or live in their own homes because they are able to take care of themselves. Few older people really need to be confined in a nursing home. The cost of nursing home insurance must be weighed against your ability to pay the premiums and the probability of need for such insurance.

You should consider some alternatives. If an indigent person needs nursing home care, the state will care for him or her with our tax dollars. But the Lord says we are to honor our fathers and mothers. The word *honor* implies financial help. The long-term solution for our society is for us to take care of our older family members (1 Timothy 5:8). Remember, if you can't afford insurance, then you have to believe that God is going to take care of your needs.

Two free booklets to help you shop for insurance wisely are:

Publication D12893
A Guide to Long-Term
   Care Insurance
AARP
1909 K Street NW
Washington, DC 20049

The Consumer's Guide to
   Long-Term Care Insurance
Health Insurance Association
   of America
ACLI Publication Request Dept.
1001 Pennsylvania Avenue NW
Washington, DC 20004

(Please include a self-addressed, stamped envelope.)

FUNERAL AND BURIAL INSURANCE

The best plan in existence to reduce burial costs is called the Memorial Society. The cost of the plan guarantees, in the event of the death of a family member, that it will provide burial at a low cost. The plan is offered through standard funeral homes. For more information concerning memorial societies, contact:

Continental Association of Funeral
  and Memorial Societies, Inc.
6900 Lost Lake Road
Egg Harbor, WI 54209
(800) 458-5563

There is also a second method to reduce costs. By going to the funeral home in advance of death, you can prepay the funeral expenses and negotiate a lower cost. If you have a burial plot and pay for it before death, the cost is much less.

A third way is to donate your body to a medical school. The medical school will use the body for experiments and will provide burial at no cost.

Other Materials by Larry Burkett:

Books in this series:

Financial Freedom
Sound Investments
Major Purchases
Insurance Plans
Giving and Tithing
Personal Finances

Other Books:

Debt-Free Living
Financial Planning Workbook
How to Manage Your Money
Your Finances in Changing Times

Videos:

Your Finances in Changing Times
Two Masters
How to Manage Your Money
The Financial Planning Workbook

Other Resources:

Financial Planning Organizer
Debt-Free Living Cassette